Table of Contents

Meet Mill Creek

"Hi, my name is Tom Austin, everyone just calls me Tom. I live in Mill Creek with my sister Esther, my mom and grandparents. My dad is off to war. We call it the Great War; it is supposed to be the war that ends all wars. You know it as World War One. Grandma and Grandpa own Austin's Market. Mom and I help run the place. Well, I help when I'm not at school. We live behind the store with grandma and grandpa.

Mill Creek is a quiet little town; although with the Riley boys, it can get pretty exciting. Let me introduce you to Mill Creek. First there is Paul Ford; he's my best friend. He has a younger brother Tim and a little sister Sarah. They live on the farm across the river on Ford Road. Rebecca Stevens lives across the river too. Her family has a farm as well. Then there are the Bakers - Gideon, David and Ruth. Their father is the Pastor of Mill Creek Community Church, and their mother is our school teacher. I wouldn't want to be in their shoes. They can't get away with anything.

The O'Brien's own the O'Brien's Inn. It's in the center of town between the church and the schoolhouse. Their son Matthew is my age. Matthew is nicknamed Sweets, because he is always eating his mom's baked goods, she bakes for the guests at the Inn.

The Smith farm is just north of town heading towards Bennington. Vera and her younger brother Daniel live there. Vera's not bad for a girl. She plays stick ball with us boys at school during lunch. She can steal a base faster than most the boys. That's why we let her play ball with us.

Joe Barnum's father owns the mill on Mill Creek. They live just on the other side of the creek. Joe is very smart. He wants to be a doctor some day.

The Muellers are from Germany. They own the leather and harness shop. Mr. Mueller makes a good pair of shoes too. His son Heinz is thirteen so he is finished with school. He works with his father in the shop. His sister Emmy is ten and his brother Schultz is five. They call him little Schultzie because Mr. Mueller's first name is Schultz. They came to America before the war in Europe. No one holds it against them that we are at war with Germany. Mr. Mueller is an elder in our church and is highly respected in the community.

The Riley farm is across from the Mill Creek Inn. They have the best soil in the county because it is river bottom soil. Patrick and his younger brother Shaun are a bit wild. They say it's the Irish in them.

Mr. Chapman is the postmaster. Mom and Mrs. English, whose husband is also off to war, are at the post office every day looking for a letter.

The Bennet farm is up the hill on Dutch Road. Mrs. Bennet is expecting their first child. Mom says she is due any day now. Whatever that means.

Mr. and Mrs. Ashworth live between the Walters and the Muellers. Mr. Ashworth used to own the leather shop. He retired when he sold it to Mr. Mueller. The Ashworths are Mrs. Ford's parents. Mr. Ashworth and my grandpa play checkers at the store.

Mr. Walters is a lumberjack. He brings the logs to the Mill to be sawed into lumber then sold to Mr. Brenner for his woodworking shop. Mr. and Mrs. Walters live on the edge of town next to the Ashworths. Mr. Walters has a team of Belgian horses called Mitch and Mike. They are used to drag the logs out of the woods. Monday through Saturday you'll see them heading up the hill towards the woods to pull logs out to be milled.

Well, that's Mill Creek. It's a great place to live, and there's lots to explore. Something is always going on here with an adventure around every corner. You might even be surprised at who drops in from time to time. Well, I'd better get back to work cleaning out the storeroom. I promised Gramps I would have it done before supper.

"I hope you will join the Mill Creek kids and me for our many adventures."

Mill Creek Map & Ledger

1. Austin Market
2. Post Office
3. Steven's Farm
4. Parsonage- Baker's
5. Obrien's Inn
6. Smith's Farm
7. Barnum's
8. Mueller's
9. Riley Farm
10. Chapman's
11. Bennett'

12. Ashworth's
13. Brenner's
14. Woodwright Shop
15. Walter's
16. Leather Shop
17. Mrs. English
18. Saw Mill
19. Schoolhouse
20. Church
21. Ford Farm

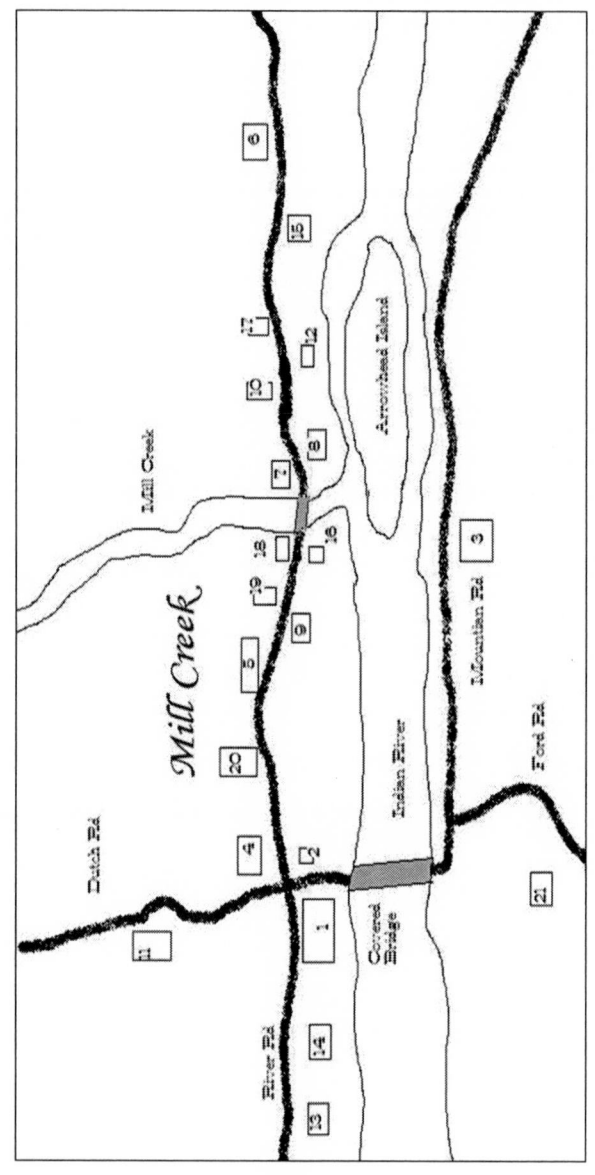

Chapter 1

Last Day of School

Excitement filled the one room schoolhouse. Soon school would be out for the summer; the children could hardly sit still in their seats. They were all thinking about what they would be doing during their summer vacation. To add to their excitement, Mrs. Baker, their teacher, said that they would play stickball after lunch. They called it stickball because they used a stick instead of a bat. The children could hardly wait for the game to start. The boys figured they would divide up into their usual teams, but this time they would have to let the girls play. They didn't like the idea much, but if it meant that they could play stickball instead of having class; they would sacrifice and let the girls play.

Tom Austin and Paul Ford were both twelve years old and best of friends. Tom, his mother and sister Esther live with his grandparents behind Austin Market while his father is off to war. Paul lives on a farm across the river with his parents, his younger brother Tim and little sister Sarah.

"I don't like the idea of girls playing stickball with us," Paul grumbled to Tom as they sat on a tree stump eating their lunch.

Vera Smith overheard their conversation, "You boys worried one of us girls will show you up?"

"Fat chance," Paul shot back sarcastically.

Vera and her brother Daniel live on a farm with their parents just north of town.

"Girls can do anything boys can do, only better."

Tom didn't say anything; he knew better. Even though she was a girl, Vera could play stickball as good as any of the boys and probably better than most of them. Paul knew this too, but still didn't like the idea of girls playing a boys' game.

"Why don't you and the girls go play your own games like hopscotch or graces?"

Graces is played with two or more people. Each person gets two sticks. Then, one of the players takes a wooden hoop and, pulling apart the two sticks, makes the hoop fly in the air for the other player to try and catch it

"What's wrong, afraid I'll beat ya again?"

"No, I just don't want to see any of you girls getting hurt playing a boys' game; that's all."

Paul knew he was fighting a losing battle with Vera, but his pride wouldn't let him give in to her. Lunch was over and Mrs. Baker rang the bell. It was time to line up in front of the schoolhouse.

"Saved by the bell," said Tom as he and Paul headed over with the other kids.

"Hey, I would have won that argument."

"I don't think so; you know she can play better than most boys."

"I know, but I don't want her to think I believe that."

Tom and Paul lined up with the rest of the children. Mrs. Baker started counting off by twos. When she finished, she said that the ones would play against the twos. Tom and Paul couldn't believe it! They were always on the same team; and now, because Tom was standing next to Paul, he was a one and Paul was a two. The other boy's weren't happy either!

"I don't want to hear any grumbling; what I say goes or we go back into the schoolhouse and write a five hundred word report on what you plan on doing for the summer," said Mrs. Baker firmly.

The boys quickly quit their grumbling, they knew Mrs. Baker meant what she said. Tom and Paul went to their teams.

"Who ist up first?" asked Heinz Mueller. (He and his family were from Germany.)

"We should flip a coin," suggested Vera.

"Good idea," replied Mrs. Baker. She borrowed a coin from one of the boys and tossed it into the air. It landed heads up. Paul's team had called heads and won the toss. They scored two points in the first half of the first inning.

Tom's team was now up to bat. He and Vera had ended up on the same team. This was awkward for him; usually Paul was his teammate. Tom glanced over at Paul as they switched positions, but Paul just headed to the outfield without looking back.

"It's not my fault we're on different teams," thought Tom.

Shaun Riley was first at bat. Pat, Shaun's older brother was catching for the twos team.

"He can't hit; everyone take a break!" yelled Pat.

"Come on Shaun, I know you can do it! Just get on first base, and we will take care of the rest," shouted Tom.

Heinz was pitching for Paul's team. He had a strong arm and could pitch the fastest of any of the boys.

"Strike one," called Pat as the ball flew right pass Shaun. "I told ya he can't hit."

Shaun swung at the next one and missed.

"Strike two."

"Time out," yelled Tom. He walked up to Shaun, "Don't let your brother tell you what you can and can't do. I know you can hit that ball, just keep your eye on it and don't listen to your brother."

"Come on, we know you can do it," added Vera.

Shaun was nervous; he didn't want to let his team down. "I can do this," he told himself. Heinz wound up for the pitch; Pat pretended to cough just as Heinz threw the ball. Shaun was distracted and looked back at Pat just as the ball flew by him, striking him out.

"I told ya he can't hit," Pat said laughing.

Shaun hung his head as he walked back to his team.

"Don't worry about it," said Tom. "You'll get it next time."

Shaun gave a little smile.

Vera was up to bat next. She was mad at Pat for the way he had treated Shaun. Taking a couple of practice swings, Vera swung the stick back far enough to hit Pat right in the chest, knocking him onto his back.

"Oops, sorry, guess I don't know what I'm doing," Vera said with a smile.

Pat got back up. "Just remember I'm back here," he said a bit out of breath.

Heinz wound up for the pitch and let it fly. Vera swung and connected with the ball sending it way out in right field. Paul ran to catch it, but it was just out of his reach. Vera was around the bases before you could blink an eye.

"Don't know what you're doing, huh?" said Pat as Vera ran over home plate.

"Guess I do after all," Vera replied over her shoulder as she walked to the sideline.

Mat O'Brien, who everyone called Sweets, was up to bat next. He got his nickname because he was always eating baked goods his mom made for the customers that stayed at O'Brien's Inn. He wasn't the most athletic of the Mill Creek kids, eating so many of his mother's pastries made him a bit overweight. Sweets stepped up to the plate.

Pat started badgering him, "Why don't you get behind me, I need a good backstop."

Sweets just ignored him and kept his eye on Heinz who was winding up for the pitch. Heinz pitched a curveball; Sweets swung and missed.

"Strike one," Pat yelled. "Guess we don't have to worry about any hits here."

Heinz pitched the ball again; it was straight down the line. Sweets swung and connected with the ball. The ball flew through the air and landed short of Rebecca Stevens who was playing centerfield. Sweets couldn't run very fast because of his weight. Rebecca, not wanting to play the game in the first place took her time getting the ball and throwing it to first base. Sweets got to first base just before the ball did. Standing on first base, he pulled a cream puff that his mother baked the night before out of his pocket and ate it. "All that running made me hungry." Everyone just laughed.

"Got any more?" asked Gideon Baker who was covering first base.

"Yeah, but I've got to have something for when I get to second base."

The next two batters struck out making three outs.

Tom's team went out into the field as Paul's team came in to bat. Paul didn't say anything to Tom as he passed him on the way in. Neither one of them talked to each other for the rest of the game. By the last inning the score was 10 to 7, and Tom's team was up to bat. Sarah Ford, Paul's sister, was first up to bat. She struck out. Tom was next, he hit a double, and Shaun hit a single after that. Vera came up to bat. The only comment Pat made this time was to tell the outfield to back up. Vera smiled as she prepared to bat. The first pitch was outside, Vera let it go by. Heinz threw the second ball right over the plate. Vera let that go by too.

"One ball, one strike," yelled Pat.

Heinz pitched it to the outside again and she let it go by.

"Ball two."

Heinz threw the third ball on the outside again.

"Ball three."

The next pitch was right over the plate. Vera was expecting it to be another ball so she let it go by.

"Strike two," yelled Pat. "Full count, three balls two strikes."

The next pitch was far outside and she let it go by.

"Ball four" mumbled Pat.

Vera walked to first base, Shaun went to second and Tom went to third. Sweet's was up next.

"Hey Sweets, want a sweet roll?" Pat said laughing.

Sweets didn't pay any attention to Pat; he was used to his rude comments. Heinz threw a fastball right down the center, Sweets let it go by.

"Strike one."

The second pitch Sweets swung and missed.

"Strike two."

"Come on you can do it," yelled Tom.

That was all Sweets needed to hear; Tom believed in him. The next pitch was right down the middle, and Sweets swung as hard as he could; putting his full weight behind it. The ball sailed right over Paul's head in right field. Sweets couldn't believe it, he had never hit a ball that far. He threw the batting stick down and started running as fast as he could. Tom, Shaun and Vera all ran in to home plate and the game was now tied, ten to ten. Sweets had rounded second when Paul finally found the ball out in the tall grass where it had landed. He threw it towards first base but it landed short, Gideon had to run out to get the ball. By then, Sweets was at third and headed for home. Everyone on Sweet's team was yelling with excitement. He was just a few feet away from home when Gideon threw the ball. By now Sweets was huffing and puffing, he had never run this much before. He saw the ball coming towards home plate where Pat was standing. "I've got to make it," Sweets thought to himself. With all the effort he could muster up, Sweets threw himself towards home plate landing right on top of Pat. This made a big cloud of dust around home plate. No one knew if Pat had caught the ball before Sweets had landed on him.

"Get off me," groaned Pat.

Sweets rolled off Pat, everyone gathered around them to see if Pat had the ball.

"Vell, do ya have za ball?" asked Heinz in his German accent.

"How could I? Sweet's pounded me into the ground!" cried Pat.

Everyone on Tom's team started cheering. Some of the boys tried putting Sweets up on their shoulders so they could parade him around the field, but he was a bit heavy for them to lift so they gave loud hurray's for Sweets instead. Pat stomped off towards home mumbling to himself about it not being fair. Tom looked for Paul and found him still out in right field.

"Hey Paul, good game huh?" "Sorry you guys lost, but we had a good time."

"Maybe you had a good time, you're on the winning team," grumbled Paul.

"It's not about winning; you know that, it's about playing a fair game and having a good time."

"Well, I hope you had a good time playing with Vera on your side," shot back Paul.

Tom started to reply, but Paul turned and walked away.

Chapter #2

Still best friends?

The sun was shining bright through Tom's window when he woke up the next morning. He was still thinking about yesterday's ball game, and Paul being mad at him; for what, he didn't know. Maybe Paul was mad because Tom's team won, or was it because he and Vera Smith were on the same team without him?

They had been best friends ever since first grade; he felt sick over the whole thing. What would he do for the whole summer without Paul? They always had great adventures collecting arrowheads and other treasures from around Mill Creek. Just last summer they built a tree fort in the old oak tree on Arrowhead Island. From there they could see most of Mill Creek. As he thought this over, Tom got dressed and went downstairs to eat breakfast.

"Well, hello sleepy head, about time you got up," said Grandma as Tom walked into the kitchen.

"I didn't sleep well last night."

"Maybe a good breakfast will make you feel better."

That was grandma's answer for everything. Food always made things seem better. Tom didn't really feel hungry, but he knew better than to turn down grandma's breakfast. She would remind him that breakfast is the most important meal of the day.

After breakfast Tom went into the store to see if he could help Gramps. That's what he and the rest of the Mill Creek kids called his grandfather. The store was attached to the house so they could go back and forth between the house and store as needed. Gramps loved children and always had great stories to tell.

"Good morning Tom," said Gramps as Tom walked into the store.

"Morning Gramps," Tom said half heartedly.

"What's the long face for? Looks like you lost your best friend."

"I did," replied Tom with his head down.

"Hmm, I suppose it has something to do with the ball game yesterday."

"How did ya know?"

"Vera Smith was in the store with her mother earlier this morning and she told me all about it. She was very concerned that she may have been responsible for the two of you breaking up your friendship."

"No, it's not Vera's fault; it's all Paul's fault."

"Oh, how's that?"

"I tried talking to him after the game, but he just stormed off."

"I see, but I rarely find it to be only one person's fault; it usually takes two."

"Well, this time it was only one, and that one is Paul."

"Ya know, there's a proverb that says pride only breeds quarrels, but wisdom is found in those who take advice. Take a little advice from someone who has made a few mistakes. Really good friends like Paul are hard to come by. Don't let one little misunderstanding come between you two."

Gramps was right; he and Paul had been best friends for a long time. Maybe he should go and try to work things out with him, but first he would let Vera know she wasn't at fault for what happened between him and Paul.

"If you don't need me in the store this morning, I'd like to go work things out with Paul."

"Well, I was going to have you help me clean the stock room, but it's waited this long; I think it can wait awhile longer."

"Thanks Gramps," Tom said over his shoulder as he ran out the door of the store.

Tom headed up River Road towards the Smith farm. He liked Vera; she wasn't bad for a girl. She wasn't like the rest of the girls; she was more like one of the boys. She sure could play ball as well as any of the boys. When Tom arrived at the farm; Mrs. Smith came to the door.

"Hello Tom, you looking for Vera?"

"Yes ma'am."

"She left for Arrowhead Island about twenty minutes ago."

Tom politely thanked Mrs. Smith and headed down to Mill Creek. He then walked along the creek until he got to the river. Arrowhead Island was located not far from where Mill Creek emptied into the Indian River. In fact, during the summer the water was low enough that you could walk across to the island. The island got its name because of the many arrowheads found on it. The arrowheads were leftover from the Indians who used to live where Mill Creek is now located. When Tom arrived, he found Paul and Vera on the shore of the river talking.

"Hey guys, what's going on?"

"We were talking about what happened yesterday," Vera replied.

Tom looked at Paul. "About that, I'm sorry for what happened."

"No, it's my fault, I got mad over something you had no control over, and Vera was just apologizing for what happened yesterday. I told her it wasn't her fault. I just got mad because we weren't on the same team, and I took it out on you."

"Well, it looks like you two don't need me hanging around. I'll head home," said Vera.

"Wait, I don't see why all three of us can't be good friends, if that's ok with you, Paul?"

"I was kinda thinking the same thing."

"Feel like climbing a tree?" Tom asked Vera.

"Do horses eat hay? Of course I'd like to climb a tree."

Tom looked at Paul. "What do ya say we take her up to the tree fort?"

"Last one up is a rotten tomato," yelled Paul.

They crossed over to the island and climbed the old oak tree that held their fort.

"Wow, you can see most of Mill Creek from up here," said Vera as she looked around.

"Yep but you can see even better through this." Tom pulled a telescope from a box on the floor of the tree fort.

"Hey, where did you get this?"

"My father gave me the telescope and this compass the day he left for the war."

Tom pulled the compass out of his pocket. "My father told me I would never get lost if I had the compass to guide me. He also gave me a Bible; and told me that the Bible is my spiritual compass to guide me through life. He said if I read it every day I would see clearly how to handle any problem in my life."

Vera turned and looked through the telescope towards O'Brien's Inn. "Hey I can see Sweets."

"What's he doing?" asked Paul.

"What else, he's eating one of his mom's pastries."

Then she looked over at the Riley farm and started giggling.

"What's so funny?" asked the boys.

"Pat and Shaun are running from Hector."

"I wonder what they did to Hector this time?" said Paul.

To answer that question they would have had to be able to see what was going on in the barn before the boys ran out. Hector was the Riley's billy goat and the boys were well known for picking on him.

They always ended up with Hector getting the best of them though.

Pat had decided that Hector would make a good bucking bronco just like in the western novel he had been reading. He had convinced Shaun to be the first to try riding Hector.

"Are you sure this is safe?" asked Shaun as he climbed in the stall with Hector.

"Sure, just hang onto his horns and pull yourself up on his back," said Pat.

"I'm not sure this is a good idea."

"Sure it is; the cowboys do it all the time, only with real bucking broncos. I read all about it in my Mitch Maverick novel. Besides, Hector's only a goat, you'll be ok."

Shaun grabbed Hector's horns to pull himself up on the goat's back. As soon as Shaun took hold of the horns Hector put his head down and shook it wildly.

"I don't think he likes this!" cried Shaun. "Open the door, open the door!" Shaun yelled as he tried to get away from Hector.

Pat threw open the stable door and started running. Shaun ran out of the stable with Hector right behind him.

"You were supposed to shut the door after me!" yelled Shaun, as he and Pat ran out of the barn. Pat was too busy running from Hector to reply.

"What's happening now?" asked Paul.

"They're running for the house," said Vera.

"Oh my!"

"What?" asked both Tom and Paul.

"Hector butted Shaun in the seat of his pants and knocked him right into the rain trough. Now he's got Pat by the britches with his horns, I don't believe it."

"What's happening now?" both boys cried.

"Hector carried Pat over to the rain trough on the end of his horns and dropped him in."

All three started laughing.

"Serves those boys right for picking on poor old Hector," said Vera.

She looked though the telescope at the rest of Mill Creek.

When she was done she gave the telescope back to Tom. "What do we do now?"

"I don't know. We have the whole summer ahead of us, and I think it will get kinda boring after awhile spying on Mill Creek with my telescope."

"Yeah, even the Riley boys and Hector would get old after awhile," said Paul.

The three sat up in the tree fort thinking up ideas about what they could do for the summer. They couldn't come up with a single idea that all three of them could agree on.

"How about we go get us a soda from the store? I'm buying," said Tom

"You don't buy those sodas. You get em for free because your grandparents own Austin's Market, but I'll take one anyway," said Paul. All three laughed as they started to climb down the tree on their way to the store.

"Well, what are you all up to?" asked Gramps when they arrived at the store.

"May we each have a soda, please?" asked Tom.

"I don't see why not, what flavor would you like Vera?"

"Grape Nehi, please."

"I know what you boys want."

"Sasperilla," they both said smiling.

Gramps pulled the sodas out of the ice chest and handed them each a soda.

Back in 1917 people used ice cut from a pond during the winter and stored in an ice house to use year round to keep their food cold. The ice would be delivered to each home by a delivery man, and he would put it into their ice chest. We call it a refrigerator today.

"Well, what now?" asked Paul.

"I don't know, maybe go back down to the river and look for arrowheads," replied Tom.

Neither Paul nor Vera thought that was a good idea. They stood around the store trying to come up with something they could all agree on.

Gramps overheard them while he was stocking some shelves and asked them if they wanted to hear a story.

All three agreed to that. Gramps was a great storyteller and all the kids in Mill Creek enjoyed listening to him tell them stories. The three sat on the floor and Gramps pulled up a stool from behind the counter.

"Well, how about the story when Mr. Ashworth and I floated a raft down the river and almost didn't make it back?"

Chapter #3

Gramps Story

"We were about your age and had been pestering our parents for weeks to let us go down the river on a raft. We built the raft out of scrap lumber salvaged from crates and other things we had scrounged up. Both of us had read The Adventures of Huckleberry Finn and wanted to float down the river just like Huck did. We wanted to have an adventure and explore the river. Neither of us had been any further downstream than Waterville and we wanted to see what was beyond it. Neither of our parents would agree to let us go. They said it was too dangerous for two boys to float alone down the river. We were determined to go, but we didn't want to disobey our parents. We finally talked them into letting us go as far as Waterville. It was better than nothing.

We set sail early on a Monday morning; the river was running slow between Mill Creek and Waterville. The plan was to float down to Waterville, pull up to shore and walk the three miles back to Mill Creek. Well, as I said, we set sail on a warm and sunny day; our moms had packed us each a lunch to eat on the way. We took our time stopping at each island looking for treasure, hoping to find something that we could bring back and show our friends. We stopped on an island at noon and had our lunch; all that exploring had made us hungry.

"What you got for lunch?"I asked Phil.

"Bread, cheese and an apple," he replied. "What you got?"

"Same thing, our mothers must think alike. This exploring and sailing downriver sure is fun, wish we could go beyond Waterville."

"I know, we're almost there and the day ain't half over yet, be a shame to stop now."

"I don't think it would hurt to go just a little past Waterville. Besides we won't be able to get the raft back home. It seems a shame to waste all that time we put into building it just to stop short of a great adventure," I said.

We got back on our raft and pushed off, floating towards Waterville. We got to Waterville and kept on going.

"What do you think the river is like beyond here?" Phil asked me.

"Don't know, never been any further than back there in Waterville." We kept sailing, not noticing the current picking up speed. Soon we were moving at a pretty good pace.

"The current is getting awfully strong. I think we'd better head to shore now before we can't," said Phil.

"I think so too."

We pulled on the rudder trying to aim us for shore, but the current had become too strong. Soon the water turned to rapids, and we were hanging on for our lives. We hung on the best we could in hopes the current would slow down, and we could get to shore.

I yelled to Phil, "I think we should have put to shore back in Waterville."

"I think your right, what do we do now?"

"Pray!"

We started praying like we never had before, confessing sin we weren't sure was sin, but we confessed it just in case. We continued hanging on for our lives and praying God would save us from our disobedience. I could just see a tree up ahead leaning out over the river. It looked low enough to grab onto if we could get the raft to float under it. We were in a strong current in the middle of the river and that tree only hung out about ten feet or so from the shore.

I yelled to Phil, "Get ready to grab onto that tree up ahead."

"We aren't close enough!"

"Help me with the rudder; maybe we can get close enough."

We both grabbed onto the rudder and pulled hard. Slowly we started heading towards the overhanging tree. Finally we got about ten feet from it. I told Phil, "Get ready to grab onto the tree!" We came to the very edge of the tree, just close enough to grab a branch. I held onto the rudder till the last second.

"Ok, Isaiah, let go of the rudder and grab a branch."

He had already grabbed onto a branch and started climbing. As soon as I let go of the rudder the raft shifted away from the tree and out of its reach. Phil turned to help me but it was too late. The raft was past the tree, and I was on my way down the river alone. I was glad Phil had made it to safety, but now I had a new problem, I was all alone and there was no one to help me with the rudder. I continued to pray and a verse came to me, "God will never leave us or forsake us." I knew He was on that raft with me, and I knew He didn't want me to drown. This gave me peace that I didn't have up till then.

By now, Phil had climbed onto the river bank and started running after me. Up ahead I could see a sharp bend in the river, but I didn't know what lay beyond that. I prayed that it was nothing this raft couldn't handle. Then I got an idea. The force of the current might propel the raft towards the shore when I came to the sharp bend. I started pulling as hard as I could on the rudder in hopes it would help get me close enough to shore so I could jump and swim the rest of the way. The raft came to the bend in the river and headed towards shore. Phil was there yelling something, but I couldn't hear what he was saying. As I came into that bend, I pulled hard on the rudder; it headed the raft right towards shore. I got within ten feet of the shore and decided to jump and swim the rest of the way. I jumped off the raft as it started back out to the middle of the river. I swam to shore where Phil was waiting for me.

"Good thing you jumped."

"Yeah I didn't know when I would have another chance."

"Chance!" yelled Phil. "Do you see what's downriver?"

I looked where Phil was pointing. A ten foot waterfall was about another fifty yards downriver. I had been so busy trying to steer the raft to shore; I hadn't realized what was ahead.

"I guess I timed that just right."

"I'll say, if you hadn't jumped when you did we wouldn't be having this conversation. I'd have to walk home all by myself and explain to your parents why you didn't come home with me."

"Speaking of home we better get started."

We walked up to the road and headed home. It took us a lot longer than planned since we had floated another three miles past Waterville. When we got home it was late, and our parents wanted to know what took us so long. We confessed to them what we had done and how it happened.

They were very thankful that we were ok; but after our moms got done hugging us, our fathers took us out to the woodshed and warmed our bottoms for disobeying.

Well, we got more of an adventure than what we had planned on. We learned a great lesson that day. It pays to obey our parents even when we think we know best; because as we learned, we didn't know best."

"Did you ever build another raft and float down the river again?" asked Tom.

"No, we knew our parents wouldn't hear of it; besides we had our fill of river adventure for our lifetime."

"It sure sounded exciting," said Vera.

"That it was; we saw lots of things. The islands were great for exploring. I even found an old silver coin on one of the islands."

"Can we see it?" all three asked in unison.

"I'm afraid not. It went over the falls with the raft. You see, I had put it in my lunch bag for safe keeping; and I didn't take it with me when I swam to shore."

"That's too bad," replied Paul.

"I agree, it would have been a nice addition to my coin collection."

"How old was it?" asked Tom.

"Couldn't quite make out the date, but it looked to be from the early eighteen hundreds."

"How did it get on the island?" asked Vera.

"Hard to say, probably one of the early settlers lost it while exploring the island. Well, it's about time for my daily checker game with Mr. Ashworth, he should be here any minute now," stated Gramps.

Just then Mr. Ashworth came in the store.

"We were just talking about you Phil."

"I hope it was good," chuckled Mr. Ashworth.

"I just got done telling the children about our river adventure."

"I'm sure they enjoyed it, I haven't thought about that river trip in years."

"Well, we better get started on our game," said Gramps.

"Yeah, I walked all the way up here for a checker game; can't beat ya if we don't get started."

"Beat me, you haven't won a game in well, I can't remember the last time you won."

"You must have a short memory because I beat ya yesterday."

"Yesterday! you know I forfeited that game because I had customers to wait on."

"You two going to argue all afternoon or are ya gonna get that checker game started?" asked Grandma.

Both the men chuckled; she had been standing in the doorway between the house and the store listening to Gramps and Mr. Ashworth the whole time.

"Guess she's right, times a wasting," said Gramps.

The two older men sat down at the wooden barrel that held their checker board, and started their game.

"You children hungry for some of my molasses cookies? I just took them out of the oven."

"Yes ma'am," all three answered at once.

The children followed Grandma into the kitchen for some milk and fresh baked molasses cookies. No one could bake molasses cookies better than Grandma Austin. The children ate their cookies, then thanked Grandma and went outside.

"Well, now what?" Paul asked.

"How about we go back out on Arrowhead Island and look for treasure," suggested Tom.

"Sounds like a good idea to me," said Vera. What do you think Paul?"

"Sounds okay, I guess."

They got as far as the Riley farm when Pat Riley saw them.

"Hey what are you guys doing walking down my road?"

"Your road, you don't own this road" replied Vera. She wasn't afraid of Pat at all.

"I do now, and you have to pay me a toll for walking down it."

"How much is the toll?" asked Paul.

He had no intentions of paying it, he was messing with him. Pat wasn't very smart so he fell right into Paul's trick.

"Three cents," replied Pat with a smile.

He thought he was going to make some easy money.

"Well, we don't have three cents; mind if we borrow it till tomorrow. Then we can pay ya back," Paul said keeping a serious face.

The other two knew what Paul was up to and it was all they could do not to break out laughing.

"Sure, but make sure you bring it tomorrow," replied Pat.

Pat pulled three cents out of his pocket and handed it to Paul, who looked over Pat's shoulder and said, "Hey, here comes Hector."

Pat didn't even look back to see if Hector was really behind him. He took off running. Tom, Paul and Vera started laughing as they watched Pat running from an imaginary billy goat.

"How far do ya think he'll run before he realizes Hector's still in the barn?" said Tom between laughs.

"I don't know, but did you see the look on his face? He must still be sore on the backside from the other day to be that scared of Hector," replied Paul.

"You are going to give him back his three cents, aren't you?" Vera asked still laughing.

"Na, I'll give it to Shaun, I figure he deserves it for putting up with Pat."

The three headed down the road to Mill Creek still laughing at Paul's joke on Pat. When they reached the end of Mill Creek where it empties into the Indian River they crossed over to Arrowhead Island.

"Boy, wouldn't it be great to find some kind of treasure on Arrowhead Island?" asked Paul.

"Yeh, it would be great; but you and I have been over this whole Island and have only found a few arrowheads," replied Tom.

"Well, what hurt can it be to search some more. It's not like we have anything else to do," said Vera.

Paul looked at Tom, "She's pretty smart for a girl." Vera playfully hit Paul in the arm.

"I'm smarter than the two of you put together."

"Oh yeah? Well, if you're so smart, why didn't you come up with the trick on Pat instead of me?"

"Why should I, you did just fine."

"You two gonna argue all day or help me search for treasure?"

Paul and Vera laughed at themselves. "I guess we are being kinda silly."

"Is there anywhere we haven't looked?" Paul asked Tom as they walked to the other side of the island.

"I think we've looked under every rock that's here."

"Have you done any digging?" asked Vera.

"No we just looked under rocks and stuff like that," replied Tom.

"Where would we start digging anyway?" asked Paul.

"I read in a book once that bank robbers buried the money under a log," said Vera. "Are there any fallen trees on the island?"

"Yeh, up at the other end is an old sycamore tree that must have fallen years ago," said Tom.

"Well, we need a shovel if we're going to dig," said Vera.

"We'll have to go all the way to one of our houses to get one," said Paul. "How about we dig with our hands? It'll save time."

The three headed to the fallen tree. When they got there Vera asked, "Well where do we dig? The tree must be eighty feet long."

"How about here," replied Tom as he pointed to the center of the tree.

It seemed to be as good a place to dig as any. The three started digging with their hands beside the log. It wasn't too long before they got tired and quit. All three sat on the log feeling discouraged about finding nothing.

"We need another island; one we haven't explored yet," said Paul.

"This is the only island in Mill Creek," replied Vera. "It would be nice to be able to explore one of the islands Gramps and Mr. Ashworth landed on with their raft."

"I have an idea," said Tom.

Chapter #4

Tom's Big Idea

"I see one big problem with your idea," said Vera.

"What's that?" asked Tom.

"Our parents, you know they won't let the three of us float down the river alone."

Tom came up with the idea of building a raft and floating it down the river just like Gramps and Mr. Ashworth had. Only they would stop at Waterville before the strong currents and waterfall. He figured they could explore the islands on the way and maybe find some treasure.

"We'll have to sell our parents on the idea," said Tom.

"How do we do that?" asked Paul.

"I'm not sure yet, but we'll figure it out."

"Lets figure out first how we're going to build a raft," said Tom.

The three went to the tree fort to do their planning. They worked on the details of the raft and the trip. They hoped that if it was well thought out and organized maybe their parents would go for the idea.

"I figure it should only take us about half the day to float the three miles from Mill Creek to Waterville and have enough time to stop on some of the islands and explore," said Tom.

"I don't like the idea of all the work we'll have to put into building the raft just to leave it in Waterville," Paul said.

"Maybe we don't have to," replied Tom.

"What do you mean?" asked Vera.

"Well, we did get the story from Gramps. He would understand us not wanting to leave the raft in Waterville. Maybe we could talk him into meeting us in Waterville. We could take the raft apart for him to haul back in the wagon."

"Do you think he would?" asked Vera.

"One way to find out."

The three climbed down from the tree fort and headed for the store. When they reached the Riley farm, Pat stopped them again.

"Think you're pretty funny playing your joke on me."

"Well, we did get a pretty good laugh out of it," said Vera.

"Your trick ain't gonna work again; I know Hector is in his pen in the barn."

"Oh, we know you're too smart to fall for that trick again, can't get any more tricks by you," said Paul!

"That's right, and don't you forget it. Now where's my money? I figure you owe the three cents you took from me last time, three cents from the toll you never paid, and I'm charging you five cents this time for the trouble you gave me. Let's see. That's a total of eleven cents."

"Ok, you got us this time," said Paul. Do you have change for a quarter?"

Pat checked his pockets. "No."

"I'll tell you what, you wait here. We're going down to Austin's Market, and I'll get change and bring it back to ya."

"Ok, but hurry up, I aint got all day ya know."

Tom, Paul, and Vera started towards Austin's Market.

"Wait," said Pat.

They turned around and faced him.

"I'll get the change out of Shaun's savings jar."

Vera was going to protest, but Paul cut her off. "Here, put the three cents I took from you in his jar. I'll bring you the rest so you don't have to get any change out of the jar."

"I'll just give Shaun the three cents. It'll save me a trip up to his room," replied Pat.

Paul handed Pat the three cents. Pat took the money and headed for the house. The three continued their walk to Austin's Market.

"He's not the brightest kid in Mill Creek is he?" said Vera.

"No, when smarts were being passed out he passed them up," said Paul.

"Well, Shaun made three cents anyway. He won't know what to do. His brother giving him three cents instead of taking it," said Tom.

All three of them laughed at the thought of Pat giving Shaun the three cents that Paul had tricked him out of.

At Austin's Market, Gramps was waiting on Mrs. O'Brien. They had to wait until he was finished. The three stood out front of the store until Mrs. O'Brien came out so they wouldn't disturb her and Gramps.

"Well, what have you three been up too?" asked Gramps.

"We came to talk to you about a project we want to do," replied Tom.

"Oh, and what's that?"

The three quickly filled Gramps in on their plan except for the part of bringing back the raft.

"It seems to me you have it all worked out," said Gramps.

"Well, not all," replied Tom.

"Oh?"

"We thought that it would be nice if someone would bring a wagon down to Waterville so we could take the raft apart, and bring it home so it wouldn't go to waste."

"Oh really, and who did you have in mind for the transportation of your raft?"

Gramps knew the answer. He just liked giving Tom a hard time.

"Well, we were sort of hoping you would," said Vera with a pleading look on her face.

It was a game now, and the children knew that Gramps was playing with them. Gramps was a push-over for children.

"What did your parents say?"

"We haven't exactly asked them yet," replied Tom.

"Don't you think you should ask them first?"

"We wanted to get all the facts together before we did that."

"Oh, I see. Well as long as your parents are all right with it; I'm okay with it."

The three thanked Gramps and went back outside.

"Now that that's taken care of all we have to do is sell the idea to our parents," said Tom.

"That won't be an easy sell either," said Vera.

"Speaking of parents, mine aren't going to be happy if I don't get going; it's chore time," said Paul.

"Yeh, I'd better go too. I should help my mother fix dinner," Vera added.

"Let's all ask our parents tonight and meet back here tomorrow," said Tom.

They all agreed, and then Paul and Vera went home. Tom went back into the store to see if he could help Gramps.

"How do you think I should bring up the river trip to mom?" Tom asked Gramps as they were stocking shelves.

"Proverbs sixteen three says, 'commit to the LORD whatever you do, and your plans will suc-ceed.' Have you prayed about it yet?"

"Well, no, not exactly."

"Why don't you pray about it, and let God give you an answer to your question?"

Tom went up to his room and knelt by his bed and prayed. After dinner he asked his mother if he could speak with her.

"After I help your grandmother with the dishes," she replied.

Tom sat at the table with his sister, Esther, and helped her put together a jigsaw puzzle.

"What do you want to talk to mom about?" asked Esther.

"I'll tell ya after I talk to mom."

"Why can't you tell me now?"

"Because I'd rather talk to mom first, that's all."

"I don't see why you can't tell me. Does it have to do with Vera Smith?"

"No, well sort of, never mind."

Tom got up from the table. Little sisters, he thought to himself as he walked into the parlor. Gramps was sitting in his chair reading the newspaper. He spotted Tom walking in.

"Talk with your mother yet?"

"She's still doing the dishes with Grandma."

"Says here in the paper that there's been a bank robbery over in Smithville Flats, says they got away with over ten thousand dollars."

"Wow, that's a lot of money!" exclaimed Tom.

Just then, Tom's mother walked into the parlor. "You ready for our talk?"

"Yes ma'am"

"You want to go outside or sit here in the parlor?" she asked.

"The parlor's fine."

He thought maybe with Gramps in the room he would stand a better chance of talking his mother into the river adventure. Tom's mother sat down next to him. "What's on your mind?"

Tom explained to his mother what he and his friends wanted to do.

"I wish your father was here to make this decision; I don't know. Dad, what do you think?"

Gramps put down his paper. "Tom has already talked to me about it. I'm afraid he got the idea from me."

Gramps told her the story about his river adventure with Mr. Ashworth. When he finished he told her he didn't see any problem with them just going as far as Waterville. He would pick them up and bring them and the raft home.

"Well, I guess I don't mind as long as your grandfather oversees this whole adventure of yours."

Tom gave his mother a hug and thanked her. He couldn't wait to tell Paul and Vera. "Hope they have the same success," thought Tom.

The next day Paul arrived at the store first. "Well, what did they say?" Tom asked Paul as they walked outside.

"My father was okay with it, but not my mom."

"So you can't go?" Tom asked with sigh.

"I didn't say that, I just said my mom wasn't okay with it. When she was a little girl, her father, (Phil Ashworth), told her the story of the river adventure he had with your grandfather. My father talked it over with her, and she said as long as your grandfather supervised the whole thing she would let me go."

"My mom said pretty much the same thing."

"Well, so far so good," said Paul.

"I wonder where Vera is?" asked Tom.

The boys sat on the front step of the store waiting for Vera. Finally, they saw her coming down the road with her father. When Vera and her father arrived at the store, Mr. Smith asked the boys, "So, you want to take my daughter down the river with you?"

"Well, yes sir, I mean uh."

The boys didn't quite know what to say. Just then, Vera broke out into a giggle, and Mr. Smith smiled.

"He's just picking on ya. I can go. My father just wants to talk to Gramps to make sure he is overseeing this adventure."

The boys sat back down on the step relieved that they weren't in trouble. Mr. Smith went into the store to talk to Gramps.

"Well I guess we had better get to work building the raft," said Tom.

"Yeah, let's get started," said Paul.

"What will we use to build it?" asked Vera.

The boys looked at each other. "I guess we haven't thought that out yet, maybe Mr. Barnum has some scrap at the mill we can have."

The three headed down to the mill. They were thankful that Pat wasn't out when they walked by the Riley farm. When they got to the mill they had to wait for Mr. Barnum because he was in the middle of sawing a log. After finishing, he asked the children what he could do for them. They explained what they were doing and asked if they could have some scrap wood to build the raft.

"Sorry, but I cut up all my scrap for firewood."

The three politely thanked him and walked down Mill Creek to the river. They went across to Arrowhead Island and climbed up into the tree fort.

"Well, what do we do now?" asked Paul.

The three sat in silence for a while. Then Tom came up with an idea. "Gramps has all those wooden crates and barrels that merchandise and hardware come in at the store. We could build the raft out of those."

The three agreed it was a good idea. They climbed down from the tree fort and headed to the store. On their way, they met Pat.

"Where you guys going?"

They didn't want to tell him about the raft because it would just mean trouble.

"Just going down to the store," answered Tom.

"What for?"

"You writing a book?" asked Vera. She was getting tired of Pat's harassment.

"Hector!" Paul shouted.

"I'm not falling for that again," said Pat.

This time Hector really was headed right for them. He had escaped from his pen in the barn and was headed right for Pat's backside. Pat never moved because he thought Paul was playing another trick on him. Hector went right for Pat. The three backed away from Pat as Hector got close behind him.

"What, you afraid of me?" sneered Pat.

Just as he got those words out, Hector connected with his backside, and Pat let out a yell that could be heard all over Mill Creek. He picked himself up and started running, with Hector following right behind giving him a butt every time Hector got close enough.

"Thank you, Hector," said Paul laughing at the sight, as the three headed to the store.

"How come you guys won't stand up to him?" asked Vera. "There are two of you and only one of him."

"It's not that we won't stand up to Pat, we just find it fun to pull one over on him," replied Tom.

"Yea, it's not all that hard to play tricks on him. Besides, it's a lot better than getting into a fight," said Paul. "Now we can yell Hector, and he won't know whether or not to believe us, he'll just start running."

"I guess you're right. We do get a good laugh every time we meet up with him."

When they reached the store Tom's mother was watching the store for Gramps.

"Where's Gramps?" asked Tom.

"He's in the stockroom putting away the Wells Fargo shipment."

The three went back to the stockroom to ask Gramps about the barrels and crates. Gramps was busy unpacking a crate.

"Hi Gramps," all three said at once.

"Well, what are you three up to?"

"We were wondering if we could have some of the old crates and barrels that you have around here?" said Tom.

Gramps looked around. "I guess there are a few crates I wouldn't mind getting rid of."

"Can we have them?"

"Sure."

Tom smiled and was about to say thanks when Gramps said "for a price."

Chapter #5

Working

Tom, Paul, and Vera looked at each other. What did Gramps mean, for a price?

"You're going to need more than crates and barrels," said Gramps. "You'll need nails, rope, some pitch to make those barrels water tight and a long board for the rudder."

"What do you mean, for a price?" asked Tom.

"Well, I think you ought to earn these things instead of me just giving them to you. The three of you can start by cleaning up the stockroom."

Tom, Paul, and Vera got to work cleaning the stockroom. They worked all week on different projects that Gramps gave them to do.

"Wow, this is hard work," said Paul as he lifted the last crate into place on the shelf.

Tom pulled the crates and dry goods off the shelves, Vera dusted the shelves, and Paul put the crates and dry goods back on the shelves.

"Dusty too," said Vera after she sneezed from the dust she had just brushed off the shelf.

"Well, I think we're done here. Let's see what else Gramps has for us to do," said Tom.

Paul and Vera followed him into the store. "We finished cleaning the stockroom. What's next?"

"Your Grandmother would like her garden weeded."

The three looked at each other. It wasn't their favorite job, but they would do it so they could earn the material for the raft. Off they went to Grandma's garden to pull weeds.

"I didn't know this river adventure was going to be so much work," said Paul as he pulled a weed from between the carrots.

"Well Gramps always says that hard work brings a profit. I guess our hard work will profit us by getting us the raft we need to get to the islands to find treasure," replied Tom.

"Any of you treasure hunters thirsty?" asked Grandma. She was standing behind the children holding a tray of glasses filled with cold lemonade.

"Boy, are we!" replied all three. They thanked Grandma and each took a glass of nice cold lemonade.

"Well, I declare; I don't think my garden has looked this nice in quite a while," said Grandma as she looked around her garden.

"We aim to please," Paul said with a big smile.

"Always the joker just like your grandfather," said Grandma. Paul's grandfather was Mr. Ashworth and also Grandma Austin's brother. This made Tom and Paul second cousins.

"I guess I got it from the best," replied Paul still giving a big smile.

"Well, I don't know about the best, but that brother of mine sure was a joker in his time. I remember one time when he tied up the school outhouse with the teacher in it."

"Why did he do that?" asked Paul.

"Mr. Periwinkle, the schoolteacher, was very strict. He used to carry a switch with him in class; if you didn't get an answer right, he had you hold out your hand and he beat it with the switch. Well, your grandfather is left handed you know." Paul nodded his head. "Mr. Periwinkle believed that all people should be right handed. So every time your grandfather used his left hand, Mr. Periwinkle would have him hold out his hand. He would beat his left hand until it left welts on his skin."

"Didn't you tell your parents?" asked Vera.

"No, Mr. Periwinkle threatened us. If we said anything to our parents, he would beat us even worse for it."

"How did it come about that Grandpa tied Mr. Periwinkle in the outhouse?" asked Paul.

"Well, your grandfather, as you know, was quite the joker. He knew something had to be done about Mr. Periwinkle. So one day, he brought some rope to school. He hid it under a bush by the outhouse. When Mr. Periwinkle excused himself to go to the outhouse, your grandfather went out after him. He got the rope from under the bush and wound it several times around the outhouse so Mr. Periwinkle couldn't get out. Your grandfather came back into the schoolhouse and told the class that they were dismissed for the day. The teacher was tied up and couldn't make it back to class."

"What happened next?" all three asked.

"We all went home."

"No, I mean to grandpa," stated Paul.

"Oh, well, Mr. Periwinkle knew who did it, so he came to our house to tell my parents."

"Then what happened?" the three asked in anticipation.

"Mr. Periwinkle told my father what your grandfather had done to him. Our father gave Mr. Periwinkle permission to give your grandfather a whipping. They went out to the woodshed to do it. I saw what was going on, before Mr. Periwinkle could start, I told my mother what he had been doing to everyone, especially your grandfather. She went out to the woodshed and put a stop to the whipping. When she told my father what I had said, he told Mr. Periwinkle to leave. The rest of the town got wind of what happened, and the men of the town told Mr. Periwinkle to leave. Mr. Jameson the school superintendent notified the surrounding school boards so Mr. Periwinkle couldn't get a job teaching again."

"What did you do for a school teacher?" asked Vera.

"My mother was a school teacher before she married my father, so she filled in the rest of that school year. The following year the school board hired Miss Evens. She was the nicest teacher we ever had."

"Grandpa never told me that story before," said Paul.

"He doesn't talk about it much; it wasn't a very pleasant memory for him. Well, I'd better get back into the kitchen, or I won't have supper made on time."

"Thanks for the lemonade," all three said together.

"You're welcome; just make sure you bring the empty glasses in when you're done," said Grandma as she went back into the house.

"Wow, that was a pretty bold thing for my grandfather to do."

"I'm glad we have Mrs. Baker," said Vera.

"Me too," agreed Tom.

Paul was thinking maybe he should tie Pat in the outhouse when school started back up. The three finished their lemonade and got back to work weeding Grandma's garden. When they finished, they took their empty glasses to Grandma. Then they went to see what Gramps wanted them to do next.

"I think it's late enough, you can be finished for the day," said Gramps. "I'll have more work for you to do tomorrow."

Tom said goodbye to Paul and Vera and went up to his room. He was so tired from all the work they had done that he fell asleep on his bed. Paul and Vera were tired also but they both had chores to do when they got home. It was the same for the rest of the week since Gramps kept them busy with odd jobs.

"Boy, I'll be glad when we have worked enough to earn all the stuff we need for the raft," said Paul as he helped the others wash the front windows of the store.

"Me too, I'm getting tired of working all day and going home and doing chores at night," said Vera.

"We should be almost done," said Tom. "I heard Gramps telling my mom he was running out of things for us to do."

They finished up cleaning the front windows and went inside to see what Gramps had for them next.

"I would say it's time to start building a raft," said Gramps when the three asked him what they had to do next.

Chapter #6

Building the Raft

Finally, they could start building the raft. They started by taking all the building materials they thought they would need down to Arrowhead Island. Six wooden barrels would be used to float the raft. Because of their extreme weight, the barrels were rolled down to the island. The crates were carried one at a time. Finally, after several trips, they got all the stuff they needed to get started.

"Where do we begin?" asked Vera.

"First, we need to draw a design for the raft," replied Tom.

"Naw, let's just build it," said Paul.

"How are we going to build it without knowing what we're building?" asked Tom.

"I guess you have a point there," said Vera.

"We throw some crates together, put the barrels under them, and there you have a raft," replied Paul.

"I don't think I want to float down the river on something we just throw together," said Vera.

"Me neither," said Tom.

"Ok, draw up the design if that will make the two of you happy."

"How about if we give it a rest?" said Vera. "We've been working hard all week; and I don't know about you two, but I'm beat."

Tom and Paul looked at each other. "I am pretty tired," said Paul.

"Me too," said Tom.

"How about if we start it on Monday?" said Vera.

The three of them put all the things they had brought down to the island, in a pile by the oak tree.

"There, that should do it till Monday," said Tom as they put the last of the crates in the pile.

That night Tom drew up a design for the raft that he thought would work. The next day was Sunday so he would see Paul and Vera at church. He met Paul in front of the church before Sunday school started. They went inside and to the back of the church where a room had been added on for the children's Sunday school. Vera was sitting with some of the girls so Tom would have to wait until after church to show her and Paul the drawings he made up the night before. Mrs. Baker, the school teacher, was also their Sunday school teacher, and the wife of Pastor Baker the pastor of Mill Creek Community Church. After Sunday school and church, Tom, Paul, and Vera all met together outside the church. Tom pulled the plans he had drawn up last night from his pocket and showed them to Paul and Vera.

"Looks good to me," said Paul.

"Me too," Vera said as she finished looking at the drawing.

Vera's mother called her; they were ready to head home for lunch.

"We'll all meet at the island tomorrow," said Tom. Then the three left to go home with their families.

Early the next morning all three met on Arrowhead Island by the oak tree.

"Where did it all go?" asked Vera. She was the last one to arrive on the island.

"That's what we were wondering," said Paul.

All three looked at where they had left the pile of crates, wooden barrels, and all the other things they had worked so hard for. It was all gone!

"Someone must have taken it," said Tom.

"But who?" replied Vera.

"I wonder if Pat is behind this?" said Paul.

"What do we do now?" asked Vera.

"I say we pay Pat a visit," said Tom.

They all agreed to see if Pat had their building materials. When they arrived at the Riley's, Pat was waiting for them.

"I figured you would be paying me a visit."

"Give it back, it's not yours," Paul demanded.

"Whoa wait a minute. First of all, what are we talking about here?" asked Pat

"You know exactly what we're talking about," said Tom.

"You have our stuff, and we want it back," said Vera.

"OK, say I do have it. How much will you give me for it?" said Pat with a smirk on his face.

"Give you for it, it doesn't belong to you!" yelled Paul. He was about to take a swing at Pat, Tom held him back.

"That's not the way to take care of this," said Tom as he held onto Paul.

Pat backed up, "Yeah, that's not the way to take care of it," he mocked Tom.

"You want me to let him go?" Tom asked.

Pat knew better; Paul was bigger than him even though they were the same age.

"Well, you can't have it back until you pay me," said Pat.

"Pay you! That stuff is ours, and you stole it from us," said Tom.

"Prove it," shot back Pat.

"No problem," said Tom as he walked away. Vera and Paul followed him.

"What are ya gonna do?" asked Paul.

"I'm going to prove that all that stuff is ours," replied Tom.

"How are ya gonna do that?" asked Vera.

"We worked hard for it, and all of it came from Austin's Market. Gramps knows it's ours because we worked for him to earn it." They reached Austin's Market and found Gramps behind the counter.

"Well, I figured you three would be building a raft today," said Gramps as the three came into the store. They told him what had happened with Pat and the building materials. "Sounds to me like I need to pay the Riley farm a visit," replied Gramps after listening to their story. Gramps got Grandma to come and watch the store while he paid the Riley farm a visit. "You three stay here and help run the store. I'll be back." With that, Gramps headed down to the Riley farm.

"Why don't the three of you get yourselves a soda out of the ice box?" said Grandma. She knew it would help them feel better.

They each picked their favorite soda and popped the lids off the bottles. Back then soda came in a glass bottle not a can or plastic bottle.

"Is there anything we can help with?" asked Vera as she took a sip of her Grape Nehi.

"No, you three have done such a wonderful job around here there isn't much of anything left to do except wait on customers."

Grandma went on to say how much she appreciated them weeding her garden. It was getting harder for her as she was getting older, and her arthritis kept her from keeping up with the weeding. The three agreed to keep her garden weeded for the rest of the summer. She thanked them and said she would really appreciate that. After a while, Gramps came back.

"Your building material is back where you left it."

"Wow, what did you do?" asked Tom.

"Let's just say when I got done talking to Mr. Riley, Pat was in the process of putting back everything he took from ya."

"Thanks Gramps", all three said at once.

"Glad to help. You three worked hard for that stuff. I don't think Pat will be bothering you for a long time. I heard his father tell him he would make sure he had plenty enough to keep him busy for the rest of the summer. Well, you three better get down there and get to work. I'm anxious to see this raft."

They thanked Gramps again, and told Grandma they would be back later to weed her garden.

"I'm glad you stopped me from slugging Pat," said Paul. "This was a much better way to handle things."

"What are friends for?"

The three worked hard on the raft. They didn't forget their promise to Grandma and came back to weed her garden for her. By the end of the week, they had the raft almost finished.

"We need a long board for the rudder," said Tom.

"Where we gonna get it? None of the boards from the crates are long enough," said Paul.

"How about if we take one of these young trees and cut it down. Then we can attach a short board on the end of it," said Vera.

"Why didn't I think of that?" said Paul.

"Because I'm a girl and everyone knows girls are smarter than boys."

"I didn't know that. Did you know that?" Tom said to Paul in a joking manner.

"Nope, never heard of that either."

"All right you two, you gonna talk all day or you gonna cut down one of those trees so we can make a rudder and finish this thing?"

The boys cut down a young tree, and chopped the top off to make a pole. Then they cut a groove at the bottom of the pole to place a wide board. Finally, they drove three nails through the pole and board to keep it in place.

"There, we have a rudder to steer our raft," said Tom.

They attached it to the back of the raft and swung it back and forth to make sure it would stay in place.

"All we have to do now is get it in the water," said Vera.

Tom and Paul looked at each other. In all the excitement of building the raft, they hadn't thought about how they would get the raft into the water. Now what would they do?

Chapter #7

The Big Day

❝I can't believe we didn't think of how we were going to get the raft into the water," said Paul.

"We'll think of something," replied Tom. "Remember our memory verse from Sunday school. James 1:4 'Perseverance must finish its work so that you may be mature and complete, not lacking anything'. We need to persevere and not give up. I know we've worked hard; now let's work a little harder and figure a way to get the raft to the water.

"Why don't we loosen the barrels and role it into the water," said Vera.

"Why didn't we think of that?" said Paul. "I know, I know, it's because girls are smarter than boys."

"I think I'm beginning to believe it," said Tom with a laugh.

They got to work and loosened the ropes that kept the barrels in place under the raft. Then they rolled the raft into the water just like Vera had suggested.

"That wasn't too bad," said Paul.

The three got onto the raft to test if it would hold all their weight. The six barrels were more than enough to hold them.

"I think we should name it," said Vera.

"Well, since it was your idea how to get it into the water, I think you should name it," said Paul. "What do you think Tom?"

"I agree, you name it," Tom said looking at Vera.

"How about the Mill Creek Explorer."

"I like that," said Tom.

"Me too," said Paul.

It was settled. The raft was christened the Mill Creek Explorer. They tied the raft to a nearby tree so it wouldn't float away. They made preparations for the trip, putting together what they figured they would need. Gramps gave them some ideas of things they hadn't thought of, since he already had taken this trip as a boy.

Finally, the big day came. All three were very excited about their adventure. They met each other on the island. The plan was to make their way down-river stopping at some of the islands on the way. Gramps would meet them in Waterville where they would dismantle the raft and put it in the wagon to be brought back to Mill Creek. The raft was packed with provisions for the day's journey. They were ready to set out.

"I think we should have a word of prayer before we start our adventure," said Tom.

He asked GOD to bless their journey and to keep them safe, then Paul untied the rope from the tree on shore and pushed them away with a pole. Tom had hold of the rudder. All three had decided he would navigate the raft. Paul would keep check of the depth of the water so they wouldn't run aground, and Vera would keep an eye out for logs and anything that they might get hung up on. They floated out into the middle of the river. The current was slow; so they weren't moving at a very fast pace which was okay since they were just getting used to navigating the raft. They floated under the covered bridge that crossed the Indian River. All was going well. The rudder worked very well; Tom didn't have to move it much to make the raft turn. Paul kept track of the depth of water with his pole. Vera kept an eye out for anything the raft might get hung up on. They left the town limits of Mill Creek without any problems. Paul could see his family's farm from where they were on the river.

"I've never been down this far on the river before," said Paul.

"Neither have I," said Tom.

"It's beautiful," said Vera.

A mother deer and her twin fawns came down to the river to get a drink. They ran back up into the woods that lined the river when they saw the raft. The three had been so busy watching the deer and her fawns that they didn't watch where they were going and ran right into a tree that had fallen into the river. The raft came to a quick stand still, Paul and Vera almost fell overboard because they stopped so fast.

Tom didn't because he had the rudder to hang onto, to help keep his balance.

"Quick Vera, take the rudder."

Tom handed Vera the rudder. He and Paul pushed against the tree branches that were sticking up out of the water to help maneuver the raft out and around the fallen tree. Tom and Paul pushed with all they had, almost falling in a couple of times. Eventually they worked their way around the tree, broke free, and were floating downstream again. Tom resumed his position at the rudder.

"Better not do that again," said Tom.

"Sorry, I should have kept an eye out instead of watching the deer," said Vera.

"We were all at fault. Let's just not let that happen again," said Tom.

They floated downriver keeping a watchful eye for anymore hang-ups. They also were able to enjoy the beauty of the river, all the wildlife that came down to drink, and the ducks that lived on the river.

"I wish we'd brought our fishing poles," said Paul.

"Didn't think of those," answered Tom.

"Probably won't have time to fish anyway," Paul said looking up in the sky at the position of the sun. "Good thing we got an early start or we wouldn't have time to explore the islands."

"Yeh, I'm glad Gramps convinced us to start as early as we did," said Tom.

It was a bright sunny day perfect for a river adventure. They floated down the river at a slow pace because the current wasn't moving very fast.

"We should be coming up on an island pretty soon," said Tom.

"Good, we can stop and stretch our legs, I'm not used to standing in one place for so long," said Paul.

"I see it! I see the island," said Vera.

Tom guided the raft to the shore of the island. As they drew closer Paul put down his pole and started looking over the landscape. With Paul not measuring the depth of the water, Tom didn't realize how shallow it had become. Vera was watching out for any trouble so when she saw how shallow the water had become she yelled to Tom, "Look out! the water is too shallow here!"

Tom swung the rudder hard to steer them away from the island. The abrupt turn sent Paul, who was intent on looking at the island, overboard and into the water. Tom and Vera both laughed at him.

"Very funny," said Paul as he climbed up on shore soaking wet.

They looked for a place that was deep enough to dock the raft. When they found a good place Tom threw Paul the anchor rope so he could pull the raft up to the shore. He then tied the rope to a nearby tree. Tom and Vera got off the raft and joined Paul on shore.

"Well, I guess we can explore our first island," said Tom.

Chapter #8

The Island

"I'm hungry," said Paul as he tried to wring the water from his clothes.

"Well it is getting pretty close to noon, why don't we eat and then get started searching the island," replied Tom.

They got their lunches off the raft and sat on a fallen log to eat. Their mothers had packed each of them a bag lunch for the trip. Tom pulled out his lunch. It was a ham sandwich and some of Grandmas homemade molasses cookies. A note was inside the bag. Tom opened the note and read it.

"Well what does it say?" asked Paul. He had been watching Tom and Vera to see if they had anything he thought was worth trading for.

"It's a note from Gramps," replied Tom.

"Tell us what it says," Paul said eagerly, he wanted to know what kind of message Gramps had written.

"It says, 'God will be with you on your trip, Joshua 1:5.'"

Tom thought back to last night and his talk with Gramps. He had just received a letter from his father that day.

Hello son,

Hope all is well with you. By the time you get this letter you should be enjoying your summer vacation. Wish I could be there to enjoy it with you. It's getting pretty rough here. Just yesterday we were on the road to Saint Petersburg and we were attacked by some German snipers. I dove into a nearby ditch for cover. It took an hour to flush them out during which time we lost several men in the battle. Hopefully this war will be over soon and I can come home. I pray all is well with you and your mother and sister. Give them a hug for me and tell Grandma and Gramps I said hello. Take care for now.

Love Dad

Tom went downstairs after reading the letter. Gramps was in the parlor.

"Heard you got a letter today," said Gramps.

"Yes sir," Tom replied in a sad tone.

"I know you miss your father very much, and I know he misses you as well. He told me this in his last letter to your Grandmother and I. Before your father left I gave him a verse. Joshua 1:5 'No one will be able to stand up against you all the days of your life. As I was with Moses, so I will be with you; I will never leave you or forsake you.' This was Gods promise to Joshua when he took Moses' place leading the Israelites. I let your father know it's also a promise to us. Your Grandmother and I are praying for your father every day as I know you, your mother, and sister are too. I know many of our church members are praying for him also. God hears our prayers and will be with your father just as he was with Joshua."

"Thanks Gramps, you always know what to say."

Tom explained to Paul and Vera what Gramps had said to him the night before. He made a mental note to thank Gramps for the note of encouragement when he saw him in Waterville.

"Gramps always has something good to say to encourage us," said Paul who was starting to dry off by now.

"Looks like a pretty big island," said Vera as she looked around.

"Yeah, it might be best if we split up to look it over," said Tom.

"I don't know if that's a good idea. I think we should stick together," replied Vera.

"Scaredy-cat! Nothing is going to hurt us out here," said Paul.

"I'm not scared; just cautious that's all."

"Well, she's probably right. It is a pretty big island, and we should probably stick together," said Tom.

"I still think splitting up is the best way to look for things."

"You're welcome to go by yourself," said Vera.

"I will." Paul got up off the log and headed for the other side of the island.

"If you find anything, give us a shout," Tom yelled to him.

Paul didn't turn around, he just waved his hand in the air as he pushed through some underbrush. The island was densely covered with trees and bushes. Exploring it would be kind of slow.

"Well, I guess we better get started," stated Tom.

He and Vera walked along the shore until they came to a tree that had fallen out into the river. It was in their way so they decided to head inland. It didn't look like many people came to the island, unlike Arrowhead Island that had many well worn trails because the kids of Mill Creek played on it so much. They pushed their way through the brush until they finally came to a stand of trees. The trees kept the undergrowth from growing. This made travel a lot easier.

"I wonder how Paul is doing?" said Tom.

"I wish he had stayed with us. I have a bad feeling about him going off on his own."

"Oh, he'll be fine."

"I hope so."

They walked to the end of the island finding nothing of interest. "Well, I guess we better head back, Paul is probably at the raft waiting for us," said Tom.

The two of them headed back to the raft. Paul still hadn't gotten back yet by the time they had arrived.

"Do you think we should go look for him?" asked Vera.

"No not yet. Why don't we go sit on that log where we ate lunch and wait for him?"

"I wonder what is taking Paul so long?" questioned Vera as they waited on the log.

"Oh, he can be as slow as a girl sometimes," replied Tom not thinking of the consequences of what he just said.

Vera pushed him backwards over the log. "I can run faster than any boy."

Tom landed on his back knocking the air out of him. While he lay on the ground catching his breath, he noticed that the ground on the back side of the log had been recently dug up.

"Hey, look at this"

Vera was still mad at him for his comment about girls.

"Oh come on Vera, you know I didn't mean you. I know you can outrun any of us boys."

Vera smiled, "Good to hear ya say it." She turned her attention to what Tom had told her to look at. "I wonder why there's fresh dirt back there."

"I don't know, but I'm gonna find out," said Tom.

They both started to dig with their hands. The digging was easy because the soil had recently been dug up. They both dug underneath the log. It was Tom who hit something hard with his hand. It looked like a metal box. Tom and Vera dug around the box until they could pull it out. The box was heavy; they brushed the dirt off, and set it up on the log.

"What is it?" Vera asked.

"I don't know, let's open it and find out." Tom lifted the latch so he could open it.

The box opened easily. It hadn't been in the ground for long; otherwise, it would have rusted shut. Both Tom and Vera couldn't believe what they saw. The inside of the metal box was full of money. Neither Tom nor Vera had ever seen so much money in their lives.

"I wonder how it got here?" said Vera.

"I don't know, but that's a lot of money to be buried under a tree," replied Tom as he took one of many hundred dollar bills out of the box.

"Are they all hundreds?" asked Vera.

"Looks like it."

"How much you figure might be in there?"

"I'm not sure, looks like thousands."

Vera let out a low whistle. "Wow, that's a lot of money."

"That's right; it's a lot of money," came an unfamiliar voice from behind them.

Chapter #9

Strangers

Tom and Vera turned around to see Paul with two strange men behind him.

"It is a lot of money, and it's ours," said one of the strangers.

He gave Paul a hard shove towards Tom and Vera. Paul fell to the ground by Tom. The strange man had a revolver in his right hand.

"I'll thank you to hand that cash box over to Bubba here," said the stranger pointing to the man next to him.

Tom picked up the cash box, walked slowly over to Bubba and handed it to him.

"Now you three just sit there by that log until we decide what to do with you."

The three of them reluctantly sat down by the log.

"What are we going to do?" Vera whispered to Tom.

Before Tom could say anything, the man with the revolver said, "I didn't say you could talk. Just sit there and keep your mouths shut."

The three did as they were told while the two strangers talked things over between themselves. Tom could just make out what they were saying.

"What are we going to do now, Butch?" Bubba asked him.

"I don't know, let me think," replied Butch.

"Wanna know what I think?" asked Bubba.

"No, I don't want to know what you think, I want you to shut up and let me do the thinking," yelled Butch.

Butch started talking to himself, trying to come up with an idea of what to do with the kids. Bubba stood next to Butch wanting to interrupt but not daring to for fear of Butch yelling at him again. Tom, Paul, and Vera watched the two. In some ways, it was almost comical to watch them. They definitely weren't the brightest candles in the house. Butch would seem to come up with an idea, and Bubba would perk up ready to listen. Then Butch would say," Naw that won't work," and go back to working on a new idea while Bubba stood silently by Butch wishing he could talk; he liked to talk. Butch started pacing back and forth as he talked to himself.

"I've got it," said Butch throwing his hands up in the air with excitement.

He didn't see Bubba right next to him, as he threw his hands up. His right hand, the one holding the revolver, hit Bubba square in the nose.

"What ya do that ferr?" cried Bubba holding his nose because it was bleeding.

"Oh, quit being a baby," said Butch handing Bubba his handkerchief.

"I've got my own; don't you remember I wore it during the holdup?" Bubba pulled out his own handkerchief.

"Will you shut up? These here kids already know too much and you go and blab about us holding up the Smithville Flats Bank aint helping any."

"I didn't say which bank we held up, you did."

"Oh, it don't matter now. They know too much; we'll have to take them with us."

"Take them with us, where we going?" Bubba asked with a surprised look on his face.

Butch took his hat off and hit Bubba with it. "We're headed south over the state boarder just like we talked about, ya dummy."

"You don't have to call me names; you know I don't like being called dummy," whined Bubba.

As mentioned before, Bubba and Butch weren't the brightest candles in the house. Some might go as far as to say their wicks weren't even lit. Neither one had completed the third grade. The only job they qualified for was working in a livery stable shoveling out the stalls. The two of them couldn't even get that right and both got fired. Both went from job to job, somehow always messing things up and getting fired. At this point they were beginning to get kind of hungry. Being that they were out of work, neither one of them had a penny between them. Butch came up with the bright idea of robbing the Smithville

Flats National Bank. Only problem was, they'd never robbed a bank before. They didn't even have a gun. So they found an old discarded revolver that someone had thrown away because it was worn out and didn't work. They figured no one had to know it didn't work. There still was one problem though. The Duke gang was in town and they were planning on robbing the bank at the same time.

Bubba and Butch walked into the bank with their handkerchiefs over their faces, and Butch holding the broken revolver. The Duke gang thought Bubba and Butch were part of their gang so they didn't even take notice at the surprised look in Bubba and Butch's eyes as they watched the Duke gang hold up the bank. In all the confusion, somehow Bubba was handed the cash box as they all ran out of the bank and mounted their horses. The Duke gang quickly rode out of town and headed north, while Bubba and Butch mounted some horses that were tied to the hitching post in front of the bank and headed south out of town. Unfortunately for the Duke gang, the sheriff and his deputies were waiting at the north end of town.

"How did you know we would be coming this way?" asked Billy Duke the oldest of the Duke boys and the leader of the gang.

"You're not the first to try to rob our bank," replied the sheriff as he handcuffed Billy. "Everyone that has tried to rob our bank has always headed out the north end of town."

"I told ya we should head out the south end of town," Billy's younger brother Bob said.

"Oh shut up," replied Billy.

"We didn't find the cash box," said one of the deputies to the sheriff.

"Well, what did you boys do with the cash box?" asked the sheriff.

The Duke gang all looked at Earl, the youngest of the Duke Brothers. "Well what did ya do with the cash box?" Billy asked Earl.

"I thought I handed it to you."

"Well if you handed it to me, don't you think I would have it? Good thing I'm in these here cuffs or I'd bop ya one," yelled Billy.

"All right, put them in the jail. They can figure out what they did with the cash box there," said the sheriff.

The sheriff and his deputies led the Duke gang back to the center of town to the jailhouse. Meanwhile, Bubba and Butch were still riding south of Smithville Flats.

"Can't we stop for a minute? I'm not used to riding a horse. My backside hurts," complained Bubba.

"Be quiet, ya bumbling idiot, and ride. We've got to get ourselves far away from here before those bank robbers figure out what happened and come after us," yelled Butch.

So they kept riding south, Bubba complaining about his backside, and Butch telling him to shut up. Riding until dark, they stopped by a river to water the horses. Bubba got off his horse walking bow legged and rubbing his backside. They started a fire to see by and opened the cash box.

"How much money you figure is in there?" asked Bubba.

"Don't know, never learnt tah count that high in the third grade," replied Butch.

"Yeah, maybe that came in the fourth grade," Bubba said still rubbing his backside. "What are we gonna do with it?"

"I don't know, I'll have to think this over. You go and keep an eye out so no one can sneak up on us, and I'll stay here and think up a plan," replied Butch.

"I'm hungry; can't we use some of that money to get us some food?"

"No, ya fool; you want to draw attention to ourselves."

"But I'm still hungry," cried Bubba.

"Always thinking of your stomach aint ya? Look in those saddle bags and see if there's any food in them. Then get out there and keep watch."

Bubba found some beef jerky in one of the saddle bags; it was better than nothing. He went up by the road and watched for anyone coming, until he fell asleep. He woke to Butch kicking him in the side.

"Can't you do anything right?" yelled Butch.

Bubba quickly got up. "All that riding made me tired Butch, you don't have ta kick me like that," Bubba said trying to decide whether to rub his backside that still hurt from all the riding or rub his side which now hurt from Butch kicking it.

"Never mind, come on, I have a plan," said Butch as he grabbed Bubba's shirt collar and dragged him back down to the river. It was now morning; the sun had just come up. When they arrived at the river, Butch started to tell Bubba his plan.

"See that island out there," Butch told Bubba pointing to the island right across the water from them. "We can bury the money on that island and when things settle down; we come back for it and head south."

"Can we keep some of the money to buy some food? I'm still awful hungry."

"No, stupid, someone might get suspicious when we show up with those big one hundred dollar bills. We're gonna get rid of those horses, head across river to the nearest town, and get us some jobs. When things settle down, we'll come back, dig up the money, and head south."

Two weeks later after getting jobs cleaning out stalls at the livery stable in Waterville, they headed back to the island to dig up the cash box. That's when they met Paul on the other side of the island. While Bubba and Butch were still arguing over Butch calling Bubba dummy, Tom whispered to Paul and Vera his plan for escape.

"Hey, you three stop talking," said Butch, who saw them whispering.

"How did you kids get on this island anyway?" asked Butch.

"We floated downriver on our raft," replied Tom.

Butch rubbed his chin in thought. "Ok, let's go to the raft," said Butch.

They all headed to the raft and got on it.

"You're going to float us downriver until we're plenty far away from here," Butch told Tom.

Chapter #10

Escape

Butch looked at Bubba. "What did ya do with the cash box?"

"I thought you had it."

Butch took off his hat and hit Bubba. "You dummy, do I have to do everything myself? You stay here and watch the kids while I go get the cash box that you stupidly forgot."

Butch stomped off to go get the cash box.

"Don't need to be calling me names," Bubba mumbled to himself.

Tom, Paul, and Vera all looked at each other. Tom nodded his head to Paul. "Ya know, Bubba, if he was really your friend he wouldn't call you names all the time," said Paul.

Bubba turned towards Paul. "Ya think so?"

"Sure I do."

He kept Bubba busy in conversation while Tom slowly got behind Bubba. With all the strength Tom had he pushed Bubba off the raft and into the water. While Bubba was floundering in the water the three jumped off the raft and back onto the island running as fast as they could. Bubba was still floundering in the water when Butch got back.

"Where're those kids?" yelled Butch.

Bubba was still too busy flailing his arms around in the water, afraid he was going to drown. Butch walked into the water, grabbed Bubba and stood him up.

"It's only three feet deep here, dummy."

"You know I can't swim," said Bubba, water dripping from him.

"Oh never mind, where are the kids?" Butch asked again.

"I don't know. I was talking to the one we first captured and next thing I knew I was in the water."

"You dummy, they tricked you, now we have to find them."

"Why can't we just float the raft down the river ourselves and forget those kids?"

Butch pointed towards the raft. "You ever operated one of those things before?"

Bubba shook his head no. "Neither have I, we need that blond haired kid to operate it for us. Besides; if we don't catch them kids, they're gonna tell the sheriff what happened. Then he and his men will catch us before we make it to the state line."

"Oh," said Bubba ringing the water out of his hat.

"I always have to do all the thinking, don't I?"

"Well, not all the thinking, there was that one time."

Butch interrupted Bubba. "We don't have all day to reminisce about the past," Butch hollered. "We gotta catch us them kids."

Leaving the cash box on the raft, Butch and Bubba went looking for the kids.

Chapter #11

On the Run

Tom was leading the way with Vera and Paul right behind him. They headed to the upper part of the island that was heavily covered with underbrush and hid there.

"We can stay in here until they pass us. Then we'll head back to the raft and head downstream to Waterville," said Tom.

"That's if they don't take our raft and head downstream themselves," said Paul.

"I have a feeling they won't leave until they find us."

"Why's that?" asked Vera.

"Well, Butch isn't the smartest person, but I think he's smart enough to realize that if they leave us we will tell the sheriff about them, and they won't make it very far."

They sat quietly, each thinking their own thoughts; none of them had ever been in this much danger before, and they were scared. Tom was thinking about a talk he and his father had up on Baldwin's Hill. He and his father used to hike up the hill every autumn to look over the valley and see all the colors of the leaves on the trees. This was the last trip up the hill before his father left for the war. Tom and his father were sitting on a rock outcrop looking over the valley.

"Son, I have something to tell you."

Tom looked at his father, the serious look on his face told Tom he had something very important to say.

"You've heard about the war going on over in Europe?" Tom nodded his head. "Well, son, some men over there want to take away the freedoms we enjoy here in America. I figure I need to do my part in protecting this country and my family, so I enlisted in the army."

"You mean you're leaving and going off to war?"

"I'm afraid so, son. You see, if we're going to keep enjoying the freedoms we have here in America; sometimes we have to fight for them. Our founding fathers thought they were worth fighting for and so do I."

"But what about mom, Esther and I, who is going to take care of us while you're gone?"

"Well that's one of the things I want to talk to ya about. You see, I'm counting on you to take care of them. Even though you will be living with Grandma and Gramps, you still will be the man of the house while I'm gone."

Tom felt a heavy burden of responsibility on his shoulders.

"Now, I know you can handle this responsibility. I've seen you with the kids in Mill Creek. You're a leader. That's why I trust you to take care of things while I'm gone. You know great leaders get their wisdom from God. It says in Proverbs, a wise man has great power and a man of knowledge increases strength. Ya know you can always draw wisdom from God's Word. Read your Bible every day, apply it to your life, and you won't go wrong. Don't be afraid to talk to Gramps. You know he has a lot of wisdom from years of reading his Bible."

Tom looked at his dad. "I'll do my best, I promise."

"I know you will, son. That's why I brought you up here to have this talk with you. While I am gone, I know you will give it your best; and that's all I and God ask of you. Always give it your best."

Tom was pulled away from his thoughts when Vera nudged him and said, "I see Gramps over on River Road."

River Road ran along the Indian River, so you could see the road in parts as it meandered close to the river every now and then. Gramps had hitched the horses to the wagon and headed out towards Waterville to pick up the kids and the raft.

Those three had better get a move on if they're going to meet me on time thought Gramps as he saw the raft next to the island. Tom, Paul, and Vera all wanted to stand up and yell to Gramps; but they knew it would give their hiding place away and Bubba and

Butch would get to them before Gramps could. So they watched him guide the team of horses down the road to Waterville.

"Well, there goes that chance for a rescue," said Paul.

Tom saw tears in Vera's eyes. He had never seen her cry like the rest of the girls. She always seemed so tough.

"I think this is a good time for us to pray."

Tom knew they needed help and he knew just who to ask for help. They all bowed their heads while he led them in prayer.

Meanwhile, Bubba and Butch had their own set of problems. Besides the problem of not being very smart, they stumbled into a hornets' nest while looking for the kids. Bubba had been following right behind Butch. As usual, he was looking at everything, but where he was going. So when Butch stopped dead in his tracks because there was a hornets' nest right in front of him, Bubba kept going and pushed Butch right into it.

You can imagine what happened next, Butch turned to run after he got knocked into the nest by Bubba. Now Bubba, being Bubba, he still didn't have a clue what was going on, so he didn't move. Because of this, Butch ran right into him. This of course made the hornets mad, and while Butch and Bubba were trying to get out of each other's way, they took no time at all to start stinging them. It was quite the sight. Those two were running around, jumping up and down, yelling, and trying to get away from those mad hornets. Finally, Butch had enough sense to head for the water. They both jumped in the water and tried their best to stay under long enough for the hornets to leave them alone. Finally out of breath, they both came up only to find out the hornets hadn't left. Quickly they both went back under the water.

Tom, Paul, and Vera heard the commotion that Bubba and Butch were making.

"They sound awful close," said Paul.

"Do you think we should move?" asked Vera.

"I don't know, I think we should probably stay put for now," replied Tom.

"I think we should move over to the other side of the island. We can cross on that side. The river is only about ten feet wide and shallow enough to cross," said Paul.

Against Tom's better judgment, he agreed to the move. They quietly and slowly moved towards the other side of the island.

Meanwhile, the hornets must have figured they had done enough damage to Bubba and Butch because they left, letting the two come up and out of the water. They both had bee stings all over them.

"Ouch, ooh, ouch!" Bubba was trying to get the stingers out from his skin.

"Come on, we don't have time for that, those kids are escaping and we need to find them!"

"But it hurts," cried Bubba.

"Quit being a baby!"

"I'm not a baby, and you don't always have to be yelling at me either; that kid with the brown hair said real friends don't yell at each other."

"Well, was that before or after they pushed you into the water?"

Bubba scratched his head. He had to think about that.

"You knuckle head, what are you taking those kids advice for? They were just trying to distract ya so they could push you into the water and escape. Who stuck with you all these years through all the tough times?"

Bubba scratched his head again.

"Me, that's who, me and don't you forget it. Now let's go find them kids."

Bubba followed Butch up the bank and into the thick undergrowth. They headed away from where the hornets' nest was and headed towards the other end of the island.

Tom, Paul and Vera were quietly trying to make their way to the other side of the island too. Neither they nor Bubba and Butch knew they were headed right towards each other.

Chapter #12

An Unexpected Twist

Bubba was told to stay a good distance behind Butch so they didn't have any more mishaps with hornets. Tom, Paul and Vera were moving very cautiously through an area thick with bamboo that was over their heads.

"Are you sure you know where we're going?" Paul asked Tom.

"I think so; we should be headed for the other side of the island."

"I don't remember all this bamboo when I came across the first time."

Tom stopped, he wasn't quite sure they were headed in the right direction. It was pretty easy to lose your sense of direction in all that bamboo. Unfortunately, he had forgotten to pack his compass that morning before he left the house.

"It's like we're in a maze with no way out," said Paul.

"There's got to be a way out, we just need to get our bearings."

Tom was beginning to realize that all his efforts weren't working and that he would have to totally give this over to God. He started to pray silently, "God I'm not able to handle this anymore please help us out of this bamboo and off this island."

Tom remembered a verse from the Bible his father had shown him. "Trust in the LORD with all your heart and lean not on your own understanding; in all your ways acknowledge him, and he will make your paths straight." He told Tom that we can trust God with everything in our lives, the big things as well as the little things. This was definitely one of those big things only God could take care of.

"Hey, I think I see an opening!" Vera shouted in excitement, forgetting she needed to stay quiet.

They headed for what looked like an opening in the bamboo. Paul came into the clearing first followed by Vera and Tom.

"We made it," said Paul.

"Yes you did," came a familiar voice from behind them. Butch and Bubba had heard Vera and hid behind the bamboo waiting for them.

"Run!" yelled Tom.

All three started running; Paul was in such a hurry to get out of there, he didn't look at the root sticking up out of the ground behind him. When he turned to run he tripped over it and landed flat on his face. Butch grabbed him by the arm and pulled him up putting the revolver to his head.

"I've got your friend, if you two don't come back I'll pull the trigger!" he yelled out to Tom and Vera.

They both stopped dead in their tracks and turned around to see Butch holding the revolver to Paul's head. Slowly they walked back.

"You should have kept running," Paul said, when the others reached him.

"You would have done the same thing for us," said Tom.

"Oh, just be quiet and get moving!" shouted Butch. "We're wasting time."

"And no funny stuff," said Bubba, remembering what they had done to him back at the raft.

All of them walked back across the island to the raft, Butch right behind Tom, Paul and Vera with the revolver pointed at them. Bubba was told to keep a respectful distance behind Butch so he wouldn't mess anything up.

Ok God, this is definitely not going the way I would have had it go, Tom thought to himself as they walked back to the raft. He couldn't understand why, when he gave everything over to God, things seemed to be getting worse. Didn't God hear his prayer, why were things getting worse instead of better? I guess I'll just have to trust you LORD and walk by faith not by sight like Gramps always tells me. When they reached the raft Butch told Vera and Paul to get onto the raft and sit down.

"Bubba you tie up those two with that rope there."

Bubba climbed on board the raft and picked up the part of the rope that wasn't being used to hold the raft in place. He cut it and then tied them together with the piece of rope he had just cut.

"Ok, you, on the raft," Butch said to Tom pointing the revolver at him.

Tom stepped onto the raft wondering why Paul and Vera had been tied up, and not him. Butch stepped onto the raft behind him.

"Ok, we have the kids, and the cash box. We can go now."

"Why are they tied up and not me?" asked Tom.

"Because you're going to navigate us down this river until Bubba and I are safe from the law."

"But there's a waterfall just beyond Waterville, the raft will never be able to make it past there."

"I don't want to go over no waterfalls," said Bubba. "You know I can't swim."

"He's just trying to scare us, there aint no waterfall."

Bubba was still worried, but he would keep his mouth shut, so he wouldn't get Butch mad at him again.

"Ok, let's get going," said Butch.

Tom took hold of the rudder. "I need Paul so he can use that pole to push us away from shore, and to keep track of how deep the water is. You need to untie him so he can do that."

"Bubba grab the pole and push us off," said Butch.

Bubba grabbed the pole and started pushing but they didn't go anywhere. "How come we aint going nowhere?" asked Bubba, all out of breath from trying to push the raft away from the island.

"You knucklehead, you have to untie that rope from the tree. Can't you see it's holding us to this island!" yelled Butch after he took off his hat and hit Bubba with it.

Bubba untied the rope thinking to himself. Well, at least he didn't call me dummy. Tom couldn't believe these two had gotten away with robbing a bank. They didn't have half a brain between them he thought, as Bubba took the pole and pushed them out and away from the island. Tom guided them out to the middle of the river where the current was strong enough to push them down the river.

"Ok, you just keep us on course and no funny stuff. You hear me?" said Butch.

Tom nodded his head and said "This was your first bank robbery wasn't it?"

"What makes you think that?" asked Butch.

"Oh, just figured maybe you two never have done this before, that's all."

"Well we weren't always bank robbers; we used to work odd jobs here and there. Times got tough and we needed to eat so we turned to bank robbing. Why you asking so many questions anyway?"

"I just wanted to know more about my captors before we all die going over that waterfall, that's all."

"I told ya, there aint no waterfall downriver, you're just trying to catch us off guard. Aint that right, Bubba? Bubba?"

Butch turned around to see why Bubba hadn't answered him. Bubba hadn't quite mastered the idea of checking the depth of the water. So when the water got deeper than the pole Bubba kept putting it down into the water. He was at the point of falling off the raft face first into the river when Butch noticed that he wasn't answering. The upper part of his body was in the water, and the rest was soon to follow. Butch grabbed Bubba by the seat of the pants and pulled him back onto the raft.

"What on earth were you doing down there?"

"I was checking how deep the water is, just like you told me to do," sputtered Bubba, out of breath. His head had been under water for quite a while.

"You nitwit, that's not how you do it. When the water is deeper than the pole you don't have to worry about it."

Bubba looked at the pole, then at the water, and then back at the pole.

"How am I supposed to know when the water is deeper than the pole?"

Butch just rolled his eyes, "never mind just set the pole down and go stand over there."

He pointed to the front of the raft. Bubba let the pole go into the water. "What did ya do that for?" Asked Butch as he watched the pole slip into the water and disappear.

"You told me to put the pole down; I just did what you said."

"If you weren't my only friend I'd push you off this here raft!"

"Well, maybe we aint friends!"

The two continued arguing with one another as they floated toward Waterville. They were so preoccupied with arguing, that when they got to Waterville, they didn't take notice of Gramps waiting for the kids on the bank of the river. Gramps took notice of Paul and Vera who were tied up and of the two strange men. It didn't take him any time to figure out those two strangers were bad news, especially the one waving around the revolver. Gramps quickly got in the wagon and headed the horses back up the bank of the river to the sheriff's office in Waterville. He quickly told the sheriff what he had seen, and what he figured was going on. The sheriff and his deputy followed Gramps back down to the river. By the time they arrived, the raft was well on its way downstream. Gramps turned the wagon around and headed back to River Road. The sheriff and his deputy rode their horses along the bank of the river, trying to catch up with the raft. Gramps pushed his horses as fast as he could, barreling down River Road in hopes to get to the kids before it was too late.

Chapter #13

The Waterfall

Tom was noticing that the current was picking up speed as they floated further down the river. According to Gramps story, it wouldn't be long before they hit really rough water. Tom was scared; he knew what was ahead, and what their fate would be if something didn't happen soon. He prayed, "LORD, I still trust in you, I can't do this on my own. I need you to guide me through these rough waters, and whatever else is to come."

Paul and Vera were praying too. While they were praying, Paul was at work trying to untie the rope around their wrists. Bubba wasn't very good at tying knots, and since he was the one who had tied them up, it didn't take much for Paul to loosen the knot and untie them. They didn't let on to Bubba and Butch that they were untied. Paul showed Tom one loose hand while Bubba and Butch were busy arguing. Tom nodded his head in response.

The sheriff and his deputy had caught up with the raft. They rode along the riverbank keeping pace with the raft. Bubba and Butch stopped arguing when Butch noticed the sheriff and his deputies on the shore following them.

"What are we going to do now?" cried Bubba.

"Oh shut up and let me think!"

Butch started pacing back and forth across the raft, trying to think of a way to escape the sheriff and his deputy. Bubba stood on the far side of the raft. He wanted to be as far away from the sheriff and his deputy as he could get. He didn't want to be any closer to them than he had to be.

The current had become very strong by now. This made the raft move along at a very fast pace. Tom was working hard at keeping the raft from hitting any large rocks, or any trees that had fallen into the river.

Gramps was rushing down River Road to reach the bend in the river. It was the same place where he had maneuvered his raft towards the riverbank. He was hoping they would remember what he had done, and do the same thing.

Tom was carefully watching the river. A tree was lying down in the water on the right side of the river. He got an idea. If he could guide the raft over to the tree, they could hit it head on, this would stop the raft. Then they could climb onto the tree and make their way to the bank of the river. It was a risk, the raft could break apart from hitting the tree that lay in the water, but it was their only hope. Tom maneuvered the raft the best he could towards the tree, but the raft didn't turn as sharp as they needed it too. They were still ten feet out from the tree and approaching it quickly. Tom pulled as hard as he could on the rudder, turning the raft hard towards the tree. The raft turned completely sideways, throwing Bubba and Butch into the water.

Paul and Vera grabbed the floorboards to keep themselves from being thrown off the raft. The cash box slid right into Paul's head while he was trying to hang on. Tom hung onto the post that held the rudder pole. The raft floated sideways past the tree with Tom, Paul and Vera still on it. The current had pushed Bubba and Butch right into the downed tree. They both hung onto the branches until the sheriff's deputy was able to climb out on the tree and pulled them up out of the water. They made their way along the tree to shore. Then the deputy handcuffed them and took them both back to the Waterville jail.

The sheriff headed down the river, keeping an eye on the children who were still on the raft. Tom managed to get the raft facing the right way again. Paul and Vera just sat in the middle of the raft, hanging onto each other. The raft rocked back and forth, making it very difficult to keep from falling off it. Tom had all he could do to hold onto the rudder and try to maneuver the raft. He remembered Gramps' story about coming to a bend in the river and using the current to swing his raft close to the shore so he could jump off the raft and swim the last ten feet to shore. Tom knew Paul was a good swimmer, they both had swam in the river many times, but he didn't know how well Vera could swim. He told them his plan, shouting it, so Paul and Vera could hear him above the sound of the rushing water. Tom pulled hard on the rudder to avoid an oncoming rock that was sticking up out of the water. The rudder pole snapped in two from all the stress of being pulled on. Tom fell onto the floor of the raft, almost falling overboard. He climbed his way toward Paul and Vera. There was no guiding the raft anymore; it would go wherever the river took it.

Gramps was praying as he waited at the bend in the river. The sheriff watched helplessly from the shore as he rode his horse, trying to keep up with the raft that was rushing helplessly downriver. It's not looking good for those kids, thought the sheriff, as he pushed his horse forward.

"We're going to have to jump and swim to shore!" Tom yelled to Paul and Vera.

"I'm not a strong swimmer!" Vera yelled back.

"We have no choice, Paul and I will help you."

Just then, the raft hit a large rock, breaking it apart, throwing all three of them into the rushing water. Tom hung onto Vera, pulling her over to one of the barrels and grabbing onto it with his free hand.

"Hang onto the barrel!" yelled Tom.

They both hung tight to the barrel, it was the only thing keeping them from going under. Neither of them could see what had happened to Paul. Hanging on for their lives, the water tossed them around, sometimes pulling the barrel and the two of them under the water. They never let go of the barrel, knowing it was now their only hope of surviving. Tom saw they were coming to a bend in the river, he remembered

Gramps story. This was where Gramps had jumped off the raft and swam to shore. When they got close enough to shore, they would have to let go of the barrel and swim for it. Tom told this to Vera, she nodded her head. The barrel swung wide taking them to within fifteen feet of the shore.

"Now!" shouted Tom as he let go of the barrel. Vera let go too and they both started swimming with all they had.

"I can't make it!" gasped Vera, as she started going under water. Tom grabbed her arm and pulled her back up.

"Hang onto me!"

Vera hung onto Tom's shirttail as he swam towards shore. Gramps waded out into the water trying to help them as they struggled, in dripping wet clothes, to climb the steep river bank. Exhausted, they sat on the bank of the river catching their breath.

"Where's Paul?" Tom asked Gramps.

"Right here," answered Paul running up behind them.

After the raft had broken apart, Paul was able to swim to shore, where the sheriff was waiting to help him out of the water. When they had all caught their breath, they walked up to Gramps wagon that he had left on the road. Tom explained to the sheriff and Gramps the whole story, from the island to the present.

"What happened to Butch and Bubba?" Vera asked when Tom was finished telling their story.

"They're drying off in a jail cell," replied the sheriff. "That was some fast thinking you did when you turned that raft and threw those two off," The sheriff told Tom.

"Well, to be honest, I was aiming to hit that tree that was in the water so we could all get off the raft and to safety."

"Well, either way, you did a swell job at maneuvering that raft."

"I'm afraid we weren't able to save the cash box," said Paul, rubbing the bump it had left on his head.

"Well, you saved what was really important" replied Gramps. "Now I think we should get you home to your parents."

The sheriff agreed and bid them goodbye. He told them he would call if he needed any more information.

On the way home, Tom told Gramps about how he gave the whole situation over to God when they were running away from Bubba and Butch. He didn't understand though, why God let them be caught by the bank robbers and then almost drown in the river. Gramps explained to Tom that God doesn't always work things out the way we think he should. He sees the big picture that we can't see. Sometimes God puts us into a situation that we have no control over to remind us to put our trust in Him. He promised us to never leave us or forsake us and I think he likes to remind us of that promise from time to time.

When the children got home, their parents were waiting at the store for them. They wanted to hear all about their great river adventure; boy did they get an earful. While the children were telling their parents the whole story, Gramps pulled sodas out of the icebox for everyone. Their parents were very glad to have them home safe and sound. After the children finished telling their story Paul and Vera's parents took them home. It had been a very eventful day. Neither one of them had to do chores that night. Their parents were so thankful that they were ok; they let them have the night off. This was a good thing since they both fell into an exhausted sleep when they got home. Tom was pretty tired himself. He went up to his room and fell asleep on his bed.

The next day the three of them met up in the tree fort. They talked over their adventure and how they would tell all their friends in Mill Creek about it. After a while they got tired of talking about the adventure and agreed they should go and weed Grandma Austin's garden like they had promised her.

Passing by the Riley farm, they saw Pat weeding his mother's garden. Pat looked up from what he was doing. He smiled to himself, he had been thinking up a plan for revenge when school started up again in a couple weeks.

School in Mill Creek may never be the same. You can find out by reading the next book in the Mill Creek series. The Big Lie.

Visit Mill Creek
@
www.millcreekkids.com

Mill Creek Kids
Book 2
The Big Lie

The Riley boys are at it again, getting into more trouble in Mill Creek. Pat is determined to get revenge on Tom and Paul for what happened over the summer. Rebecca Stevens sees her opportunity to pull Vera Smith into Pat's plan for Tom and Paul. Together Pat and Rebecca tell a big lie that causes Mill Creek to take sides. Shaun knows the truth but is afraid to tell it. Read and find out how the truth finally comes out and what effect it has on Mill Creek.

9 781606 479476